Pebble® Plus

How to Make a
Mystery
Smell Balloon

Hands-On
SCIENCE
FUN

by Lori Shores
Consulting Editor: Gail Saunders-Smith, PhD

Consultant: Ronald Browne, PhD
Department of Elementary & Early Childhood Education
Minnesota State University, Mankato

CAPSTONE PRESS
a capstone imprint

Pebble Plus is published by Capstone Press,
1710 Roe Crest Drive, North Mankato, Minnesota 56003.
www.capstonepub.com

Library of Congress Cataloging-in-Publication Data
Shores, Lori.
  How to make a mystery smell balloon / by Lori Shores.
    p. cm.—(Pebble plus. Hands-on science fun)
  Summary: "Simple text and full-color photos instruct readers how to make a mystery smell balloon and explain the
science behind the activity"—Provided by publisher.
  Includes bibliographical references and index.
  ISBN 978-1-4296-4494-5 (library binding)
  ISBN 978-1-4296-5579-8 (paperback)
  ISBN 978-1-5435-3592-1 (saddle stitch)
  1. Science—Experiments—Juvenile literature. I. Title. II. Series.
  Q164.S497 2011
  507.8—dc22   2010009483

Editorial Credits
Jenny Marks, editor; Juliette Peters, designer; Eric Manske, production specialist; Sarah Schuette,
    photo shoot direction; Marcy Morin, photo scheduler

Photo Credits
Capstone Studio/Karon Dubke, all

Note to Parents and Teachers

The Hands-On Science Fun set supports national science standards related to physical science.
This book describes and illustrates making a mystery smell balloon. The images support early
readers in understanding the text. The repetition of words and phrases helps early readers
learn new words. This book also introduces early readers to subject-specific vocabulary words,
which are defined in the Glossary section. Early readers may need assistance to read some
words and to use the Table of Contents, Glossary, Read More, Internet Sites, and Index sections
of the book.

Printed in China.
005962

Table of Contents

Safety Note:
Please ask an adult for help in making your mystery smell balloon.

Getting Started

What's that smell?

Only you will know that

it's a mystery smell balloon.

Your friends won't believe

their noses!

Here's what you need:

1 latex balloon

fork

1 clove of garlic

ribbon
or string

small funnel

Other smells to try:

1 teaspoon (5 mL) vanilla extract
1 teaspoon (5 mL) pickle juice
crushed onion

5

Making the Secret Smell

Peel the skin off

the clove of garlic.

Crush the clove with the fork.

The garlic will be squished

and juicy.

Slide the small end
of the funnel in the
opening of the balloon.

Carefully dump the wet
garlic down the funnel.

Next, blow up the balloon

as big as you can.

Tie the end of the balloon

and shake it around.

Sneak into a crowded room.
Tie the balloon to a chair
or doorknob using a ribbon.

Now watch as your friends
notice the smell!

How Does It Work?

Smelly things give off

tiny pieces called molecules.

They are too small to see.

You smell garlic when the

molecules reach your nose.

Garlic molecules
pass through tiny holes
in the balloon.

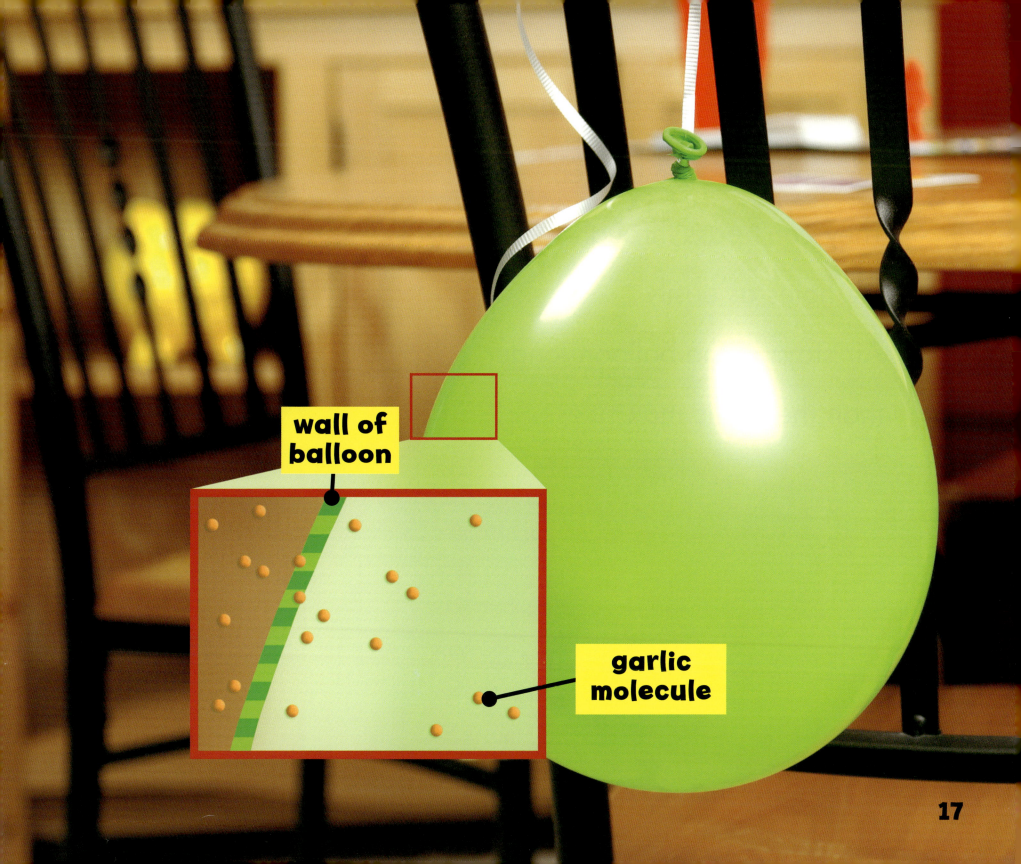

wall of balloon

garlic molecule

17

Air molecules are bigger.
They can't pass through
the holes as easily.
Air stays in the balloon longer
than the garlic molecules.

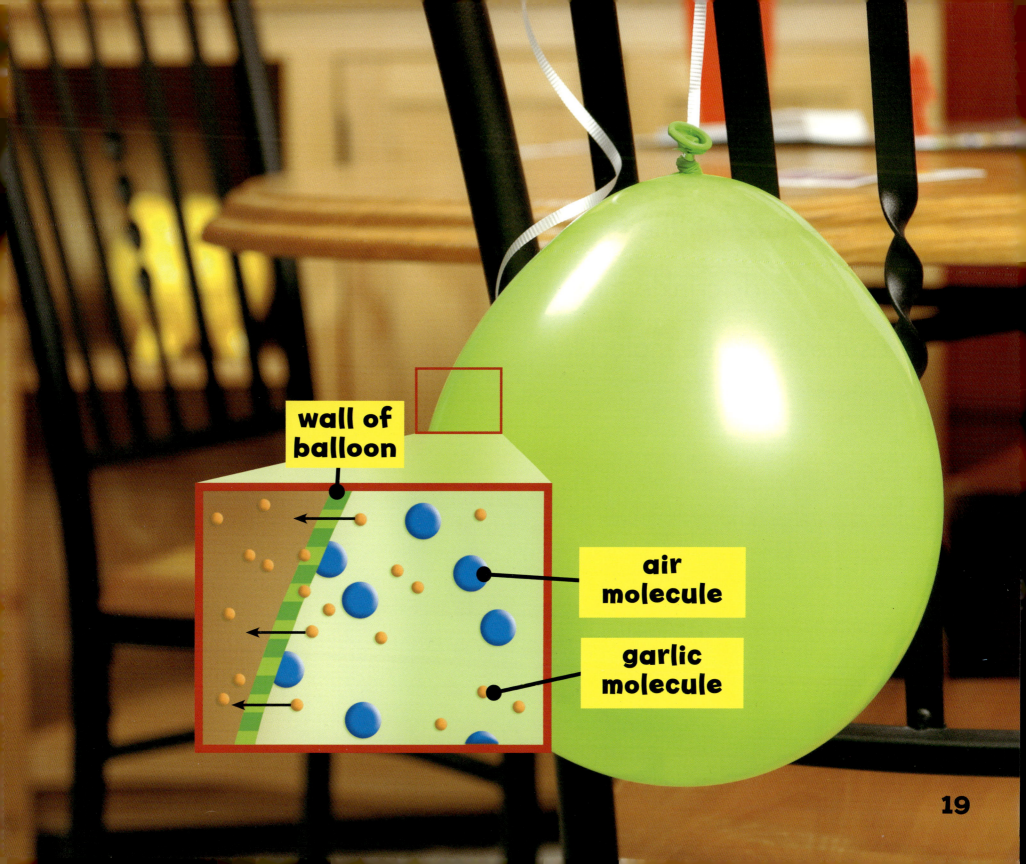

wall of balloon

air molecule

garlic molecule

The tiny garlic molecules
spread through the air.
Your friends crinkle their noses
as they sniff the molecules.

Glossary

clove—one of the sections of a bulb of garlic

crinkle—to wrinkle up

funnel—an open cone that narrows to a tube

molecule—the smallest part of an element that can exist and still keep the characteristics of the element

peel—to remove the outer skin

Read More

Ardley, Neil. *101 Great Science Experiments*. New York: DK Pub., 2006.

VanCleave, Janice Pratt. *Janice VanCleave's Big Book of Play and Find Out Science Projects*. New York: Jossey-Bass, 2007.

Williams, Zella. *Experiments with Solids, Liquids, and Gases*. Do-It-Yourself Science. New York: PowerKids Press, 2007.

Internet Sites

FactHound offers a safe, fun way to find Internet sites related to this book. All of the sites on FactHound have been researched by our staff.

Here's all you do:

Visit *www.facthound.com*

Type in this code: 9781429644945

Index

Word Count: 177

Grade: 1

Early-Intervention Level: 22